Sports Series

The Humorous Side of Major League Baseball

Bizarre Plays
Baseball Humor
Brawls
Ejections
Funny Stories
Gaffes
Knotty Problems
Quips
Rhubarbs
Tough Calls

The Humorous Side of Major League Baseball

Copyright © 2010 by Steve Boga

The Humorous Side of Major League Baseball

Thanks to my grandmother, Alcy Berg, for making available all those *Saturday Evening Posts*, for bookmarking the "So You Think You Know Baseball" columns, and for letting me watch many a Yankees-Dodgers World Series game.

And to my childhood playmates, always willing to choose up sides.

I'm also grateful to the Northern Coast Officials Association and to the umpires who helped elevate my game, including Willie Rossi, Jerry Klonsky, Monte Morgan, Ed Deibert, Jim Corbett, Jim Cuneo, Dave Hamley, Bill Kinnamon, John McSherry, Nick Bremigan, and Charlie Williams.

A baseball fan is a spectator sitting
500 feet from home plate
who can see better than an umpire standing 5 feet away.

—Author unknown

Preface

Growing up in the fifties, I loved spending nights at Grandma's house. One of the highlights was reading the *Saturday Evening Post*. She'd have them stacked on the coffee table for me, the three or four issues that had arrived since my last visit. Then after dinner and canasta, I'd sit in her rocking chair, pick up the first magazine and immediately thumb to the column entitled "So You Think You Know Baseball," which she had earmarked for me. It offered a new knotty problem every issue, most of them Major League plays. I loved trying to divine the correct ruling before looking at the answer, though I rarely succeeded.

Apparently I wasn't the only fan of that column. One of the "solutions" prompted 7,000 letters of protest to the magazine. And after the series died in 1961, the plays were compiled into a book that sold 500,000 copies.

Throughout my childhood and for much of my adulthood, baseball was central to my life. For years, I played ball every summer day and tossed, traded, and collected baseball cards. Baseball was the organizing principle, the glue, that bonded my male relationships.

After high school, forced to accept that I would never play shortstop for the New York Yankees, I hung up my glove. In 1972, I moved to Santa Rosa, California, to earn a teaching credential at Sonoma State University. Needing part-time work, I responded to a want-ad placed by the local officials association. Two years later, I was umpiring anything I could get, including high-school and summer-league baseball, and fastpitch and slowpitch softball.

In my third season, my mentor, Willie Rossi, said to me one day, "You should go to the umpire school. You could make it."

Until 1975, anyone aspiring to umpire in the Major Leagues had to attend a month-long umpire school in Florida. That year, a school opened in Reseda, California, north of Los Angeles. I took it as a sign and enrolled. Did well; got a job in the minors.

After two seasons in the California League and one in the Texas League, I was advancing as quickly as any umpire in professional baseball. But I knew I couldn't go on. Although I loved the three hours on the field—still the best I've ever been at anything—I slogged through the 21 hours off the field.

That season in the Texas League was a six-month grind away from loved ones, an endless array of hotels, restaurants, and dressing rooms, interspersed every three or four days with a grueling road trip to Little Rock or Tulsa or San Antonio.

I quit professional baseball and went home to write about that Texas League season. On many a scorching afternoon in Shreveport or Jackson or Amarillo, I had found refuge in public libraries, amusing myself by researching the humorous side of baseball. I wove the stories of my travels through the South with partner Charlie Williams with anecdotes of the Men in Blue. It's entitled *Dress Blues and Tennis Shoes*, and you can read installments of that story at www.howtoumpirebaseball.com.

For the next dozen years I umpired major college baseball, including the Pac 10, and world-class fastpitch softball. Meanwhile, I taught others to umpire, running countless indoor and outdoor training clinics.

But this volume is not an instructional guide to umpiring. (You can find that in my book *How to Umpire Baseball and Softball*, and on my DVD, entitled *You Be the Judge*.)

Instead, this is a lighthearted romp through more than a century of baseball history—with an emphasis on umpires and humor. It is also a reflection of my lifelong love affair with baseball's rhubarbs, quips, knotty problems, and strange plays. Enjoy.

The Humorous Side of Major League Baseball

Contents

I. Tough Calls

When I started umpiring, I heard the toughest call
was the half-swing.
Actually, it's throwing someone out after
you've blown the call.

—American League umpire Bill Kinnamon

In May 1901, while playing with Omaha, Frank Genins struck out and hit a home run in the same at-bat. The catcher failed to catch the third strike and the ball bounced out of play. The ump awarded Genins four bases, redefining "cheap home run."

*　　*　　*

In 1910, the baseball diamond in Harrison, New Jersey, sat right next to a train station. In the sixth inning, with the bases loaded and a slugger at the plate, a train pulled out of the station bound for Hoboken. At that moment the pitcher pitched and the batter connected, driving the ball deep to leftfield. The outfielder turned and sprinted after the ball. Any chance he had to catch it ended when the train's engineer warned him off by tooting his whistle.

Then, to everyone's amazement, the ball dropped into the smokestack of the departing locomotive.

All eyes fell on the umpire. "All four runs count," he announced. "That smokestack was in fair territory when the ball went into it."

*　　*　　*

A similar play occurred in 1911 in Mobile, when Johnny Bates hit a towering pop fly near second base that lodged in the fuselage of a passing plane. The umpire ruled it a home run, saying, "The last time I saw the ball, it was traveling out of the park in fair territory."

*　　*　　*

One day in 1912, Washington's Germany Schaefer appeared in the coaching box holding a huge bag of popcorn. As he chewed, he gazed up at the sky or out into the crowd, trying to convey his contempt for the proceedings. Umpire Silk O'Laughlin ejected him for "detracting from the dignity of the national pastime," possibly the only time someone has been tossed for eating popcorn.

*　　*　　*

Billy Evans was behind the plate one day when the batter hit a dribbler down the first-base line. The ball loafed along the chalk, then drifted into foul territory.

"Foul ball!" cried Evans.

It was a premature ejaculation. Still rolling, the ball hit a pebble and limped back into fair territory, where it died. Out of the dugout spilled the offended team, vociferously pleading their case.

The manager pointed at the ball. "Look at that, willya? How can that be foul?"

"It certainly looks fair," Evans admitted. "It would have been a fair ball yesterday, and it will be a fair ball tomorrow, and for all the years to come. But right now it's foul, 'cause that's the way I called it!"

*   *   *

One day, with two umpires on the field, and a runner on second base, batter Johnny Moore hit a grounder to the shortstop, who fielded it and cocked to throw to first.

Base umpire Larry Goetz, anticipating the throw would go there, turned and faced the first-base bag. The batter-runner was still two steps away when Goetz heard what he thought was the sound of the ball pounding into the first baseman's glove. He calmly signaled out and was surprised when Moore exploded.

"Larry," Moore said, mustering his composure, "I feel I have a right to argue. The first baseman doesn't have the ball. They made the play at third instead."

*   *   *

In a 1940 game between Jersey City and Montreal, a Jersey hitter bunted down the third-base line. While the Montreal third baseman hovered over the slow-roller, hoping to touch it once it went foul, two runners scored. Seeing that the ball would not drift foul, the infielder got down on his knees, took in a mouthful of air, and blew the ball across the line. The umpire called it foul and sent the runners back.

*   *   *

During a game in Washington, Carl Sawyer reached first. When the next hitter singled to left, Sawyer rounded second and headed for third. The third baseman took the throw squarely in the basepath, about four feet up the line toward second. Sawyer was sure to be out. As the infielder stooped to catch the throw, Sawyer went airborne, turned a neat somersault, and landed feet-first on third base.

Umpire Silk O'Loughlin, momentarily taken aback, hesitated, then cried, "Yer out!"

Sawyer leapt to his feet and vigorously demanded an explanation.

O'Loughlin complied, just as soon as he thought of one. "You left the basepath and that ain't legal," he said.

*   *   *

Umpire Beans Reardon once signaled "out" and hollered "safe" on Richie Ashburn sliding into third. When Ashburn asked why, Beans did the best he could: "It's true that you heard me call you safe. But it's equally true that thirty thousand fans saw me call you out. Therefore, yer out!"

*   *   *

On at least one occasion an umpire was put to death after working a ballgame. In Carson City, Nevada, a condemned murderer named Casey was granted a last request and allowed to umpire a baseball game in the prison yard. Instead of a post-game shower and beer, he faced a firing squad.

*   *   *

Umpire George Majerkurth, former prizefighter and football player, was a bear of a man and prone to fisticuffs. Once while working in the minor leagues, he invited an antagonistic manager to duke it out after the game. Majerkurth decked the manager in the first round, and next morning the fight was splashed all over the newspapers.

That afternoon Majerkurth didn't show up at the ballpark. His fellow umpire was bewildered: If George had been suspended, the league would have sent a replacement.

As it turned out, Majerkurth had received a telegram from the league president:

WIRE FULL REPORT ON FIGHT STOP WORK TODAY

So he did.

*　　*　　*

Before the start of the 1945 season, umpires received special instructions on how to decide catches by St. Louis Browns outfielder Pete Gray.

Gray had only one arm.

After making a catch, he would somehow secure the ball against his chest, remove his glove and tuck it under the stub, then draw his arm back across his chest until the ball rolled back into his hand, ready for a throw.

League president Harridge instructed the umpires to credit the catch if Gray dropped the ball after starting the process of removing his glove.

*　　*　　*

On August 19, 1951, a midget named Eddie Gaedel pinch-hit for the St. Louis Browns.

Weighing all of 65 pounds (29.5 kg), and standing 3 feet 7 inches (1.09 m) tall, Gaedel's appearance was a publicity stunt cooked up by Browns' owner, Bill Veeck. Gaedel wore elf shoes and a uniform bearing the number "⅛".

Immediately suspicious, umpire Ed Hurley called the managers out for a conference. Gaedel's contract was produced and scrutinized, and he was eventually allowed to hit. Under strict orders not to swing and with a vertical strike zone estimated at 1.5 inches, he walked on four pitches. The next day the league invalidated Gaedel's contract.

*   *   *

One afternoon Giants second baseman Eddie Stanky positioned himself behind the pitcher and began waving his arms like a deranged cheerleader, a blatant attempt to distract the batter. Umpire Lon Warneke ejected Stanky for conduct detrimental to baseball.

*   *   *

The Cardinals were playing the Cubs at Wrigley Field one day in the 1950s. With Stan Musial batting, the next pitch was high for ball four and got by the catcher, Sammy Taylor.

Instead of chasing the ball, Taylor stayed to argue that the pitch tipped the bat and should be called foul.

Then three things happened at about the same time: 1) Shortstop Alvin Dark ran to the backstop to retrieve the ball, 2) catcher Taylor asked for and received a new ball from umpire Delmore, and 3) Musial headed for second base.

Seeing this, both Dark and Taylor threw to second. Dark's throw nipped a sliding Musial while Taylor's throw sailed into centerfield. Musial, seeing the overthrow, got up and ran to third.

Not surprisingly, pandemonium reigned. Two balls in play is, in most sports, an officiating faux pas, and baseball is no exception. That umpire Delmore himself had placed the second ball in play made matters worse. What saved Delmore's career, and possibly his life, was that Musial had been tagged out with the original ball.

* * *

By the time Emmett Ashford was promoted to the American League, his eyesight was failing.

My instructor Bill Kinnamon was umpiring with Ashford one day in Baltimore, 1969, when Ashford's myopia got the crew into deep trouble. Ken McMullen of the Senators hit a sinking liner toward Oriole outfielder Don Buford, who charged and made a great catch.

Ashford, who was near second base, waved it off—no catch—disagreeing with almost every other witness to the play, including his partners. After conferring, the umpires changed the call to a catch. But that meant the runners, now on second and third, had failed to tag up. When the ball was put back in play, Baltimore appealed at both second and first for a triple play.

"Jee-sus Christ, what a shithouse," Kinnamon recalled. "We tossed at least three that day, including Nellie Fox . . . It's too damn bad. Emmett was a hell of a nice guy and a good umpire. They should've brought him up earlier, when he deserved it."

* * *

One of the most famous calls—actually a no-call—occurred in the third game of the 1975 World Series between the Cincinnati Reds and Boston Red Sox. In the bottom of the tenth inning, with a runner on first, batter Ed Armbruster dropped a bunt in front of home plate.

The ball bounced high in the air, and as catcher Carlton Fisk moved forward to field it, he brushed against Armbruster, who had hesitated a split second before starting for first.

Plate umpire Barnett did not raise his arms, did not kill the play. Fisk fielded the bunt cleanly and fired to second. The throw sailed into centerfield and the runners advanced to second and third.

The Red Sox manager stormed out spouting his opinion that Armbruster should be out for interference. The storm dissipated quickly, however, when Barnett asserted that it was a judgment call. As everyone knows, you can't protest a judgment call.

Actually, it was a rule interpretation. Although Barnett received hate mail over this play, including death threats (the Red Sox lost the game), fans were unaware that the league had added an amendment to rule 7.06(a) and sent it to the umpires: "When a catcher and a batter-runner going to first base have contact when the catcher is fielding the ball, there is generally no violation and nothing should be called."

*   *   *

One of the toughest calls for an umpire arises when a pitcher is accused of adulterating the baseball with spit or some abrasive element. Don Sutton was reputed to favor sandpaper. One afternoon, umpire Doug Harvey thought he caught him in the act. When he marched out to the mound and demanded to inspect Sutton's glove, the pitcher immediately complied. Harvey found paper in the glove all right, but it wasn't sandpaper. Harvey unfolded it and read, "You're getting warm, but it's not here."

*   *   *

Only once in my career did I have opposing managers on the field arguing calls at the same time. It occurred in San Jose, 1975, Charlie Williams's and my rookie season in the California League.

Seventh inning, one out, runners on second and third. Duane Murphy of Modesto hits a sinking liner to left. The outfielder charges and short-hops the ball. Charlie, on the bases, surprises me and about two thousand fans by thrusting his right arm into the air and calling "Catch!" Two outs.

"Uh oh," cries my inner voice.

"Buzz, buzz, buzz," goes the crowd.

The runner from second, caught off the bag on what is now a catch, tries to retreat, but the throw to second beats him for the third out. Meanwhile, the runner from third has tagged and touched home plate before the third out was made. I signal to the pressbox to count the run.

Modesto manager Rene Lachemann sprints out to the infield to argue Charlie's catch call. While they go chin to chin, San Jose manager Gomer Hodge visits me at home plate, demanding an explanation in his inimitable Carolina accent. "How the hail can that be a run when the last out was made by a damn force play."

"Your premise is faulty."

"My what?!"

"It's not a force play. It just looks like one because they didn't have to tag him at second. But it's not a force—it's a special case."

"Spec-y-all case, my arse."

"Maybe so, but the run still counts."

"Way-ell, then Ah'm protesting the game."

Now I have to signal up to the pressbox that the game is being played under protest. When they announce it over the P.A., the jeers of the home crowd rain down on me. Back behind home plate, I start to second- and third-guess myself: Did I get it right? . . . I know I read that play some-where . . . What if I blew it?

My concentration wanders and I miss a pitch; nobody else seems to notice.

During a pitching change, Charlie gets the clubhouse boy to fetch a rulebook. In between innings, while he is thumbing through the book, Gomer sidles up to me and says, "Yo, Steve . . . y'all getting much pussy lately?"

I eye him suspiciously. "Why do you ask?"

"Well, sheee-it, I figured we just got screwed, and I was wonderin' how y'all was doin'."

* * *

The first instant-replay call in World Series history not only turned a double into a home run, it turned the game around for the New York Yankees. With the Yankees down three runs in the fourth, Mark Teixeira walked and Alex Rodriguez drove the ball deep into the rightfield corner. He stopped at second with an apparent double after the ball ricocheted back onto the field. Video replays, however, showed the ball struck the lens of a TV camera anchored just above the fence at the 330-foot sign. Umpires changed the call. Instant replay is currently allowed only for disputed home runs.

II. Brawls and Brouhahas

You're blind, ump
You're blind, ump
You must be out of your mind, ump.

—From "Six Months Out of Every Year,"
in *Damn Yankees*

1884: During a game in Philadelphia, umpire McKean, who had been relentlessly tormented by the fans, picked up a bat, walked to the rightfield fence, and hurled it into the stands, striking a fan. The crowd erupted and tried to storm the field, but the police intervened, saving McKean from a lynching but not from arrest after the game. A howling mob followed McKean and the arresting officers to the police station.

*   *   *

1894: At Boston's South End Grounds, a fight broke out between Baltimore's John McGraw and Boston's Tommy Tucker. Somehow a fire started in the rightfield stands, possibly caused by a tossed cigarette.

The fire burned the park to the ground, then spread into the city, eventually destroying or severely damaging 170 buildings and leaving 1,900 homeless.

* * *

1896: In a New Jersey game between the Clifton and Little Falls teams, a pitcher named Connelly became so enraged over the ball-and-strike calls of umpire Mahoney that he grabbed a bat and started for Mahoney. Whereupon the umpire reached into an inside coat pocket and pulled out a revolver. Shoving it into the pitcher's face, he ordered him back to the mound. The records show that Connelly complied.

* * *

1906: The most peaceful baseball game ever played might have been Alturas (California) vs. Cedarville. An intense rivalry, it had erupted into violence in the past. On this day, the umpire, whose name is lost to us, issued a stern pregame warning: ". . . No fighting! And no hollering at me! Get that straight! The first bird who steps out of line will have me to deal with—and I mean business."

When the umpire took his position on the field, he had a hip pocket full of blackjacks and a gun stuck in his belt.

* * *

1912: Ty Cobb jumped into the stands and beat a taunting fan senseless. The private police assigned to Highlander ballpark refused to arrest Cobb, but umpire Silk O'Loughlin ejected him from the game. When league president Ban Johnson, who had witnessed the incident, suspended Cobb, the Detroit Tiger players signed a letter threatening to strike unless the suspension was lifted.

The suspension was not lifted, and the next day the Tigers refused to take the field against Philadelphia. Rather than forfeit and have to pay a $5,000 fine, the Tigers owner assembled a team of amateurs. Word went out that "any ballplayer who can stop a grapefruit from rolling uphill, or hit a bull in the pants with a bass fiddle has got a chance to go direct . . . to the Detroits."

Detroit lost 24-2. One sportswriter described some of the temporary players as "so old they could sleep in a swamp without mosquito netting."

* * *

9/16/07: During a game between the St. Louis Browns and Detroit Tigers, an angry fan hurled a pop bottle from the stands of Sportsman's Park, fracturing the skull of umpire Billy Evans. The *New York Times* described the incident as "one of the most disgraceful scenes ever witnessed on a ball field." While Evans lay on his "death bed"—he eventually recovered—league president Ban Johnson ordered the owners to police their stands or face heavy fines.

* * *

1909: During a rhubarb, umpire Tim Hurst spat in the face of A's second baseman Eddie Collins. Hurst might have kept his job if he'd said he was sorry. But he wasn't sorry. When asked why he did it, he said, "I don't like college boys."

* * *

1921: Billy Evans was calling balls and strikes when Ty Cobb, as was his habit, disputed one of Evans's calls. Cobb threatened to whip Evans "right at home plate," which would have meant Cobb's immediate suspension. Instead, Evans invited Cobb to the umpire's dressing room after the game, and before long the two men were brawling beneath the stands while players from both teams looked on.

According to some accounts, many of Cobb's Tiger teammates "rooted" for Evans. Both men had agreed not to
report the incident, but word eventually reached league
president, Ban Johnson. Cobb was suspended for one
game, while Evans worked the next several games in
bandages.

*   *   *

1940: At Ebbets Field, umpire George Majerkurth called
the last out in a ten-inning Dodgers loss. Before
Majerkurth could leave the field, a fan jumped out of the
stands, wrestled George to the ground, and pummeled him
while the crowd laughed and cheered. The assailant was
about half Majerkurth's size, and the photos of the fight in
next day's papers were no small embarrassment to the big
umpire.

The attacker, it turned out, was an ex-con on parole for a
petty larceny rap. Two years later he came before the same
judge he'd drawn in the Majerkurth case. The charge this
time was pickpocketing. All through the trial, the judge
tried to place that familiar face. Finally it hit him.

"Ebbets Field," he said. "You're the one who attacked
Majerkurth."

"T'was me indeed," he said.

The judge asked him why. "Surely you weren't that upset over the game?"

"Well, just between you and me, judge," the little man confessed, "I had a partner in the stands and we wuz doin' a little business that day. While I created the diversion, he lifted the wallets."

* * *

1945: A's catcher Charlie "Greek" George punched an umpire in the face and was banned for life from the Major Leagues, though he was permitted to play in the minors. It's doubtful George could have risen higher anyway because: 1) he hit less than .200, and 2) he was apparently a mental minor leaguer as well. When George threw the punch, the umpire was wearing his mask.

* * *

1946: One day plate umpire Red Jones cautioned White Sox pitcher Joe Haynes for throwing a beanball at batter Ted Williams. Soon someone from the White Sox dugout began to chip away at the umpire.

Jones ejected two players, but the taunting continued. He ejected five more players, but the same voice harangued him. Finally, in frustration, he cleared the bench; still the voice was not silenced.

The umpire was being roasted by an accomplished ventriloquist seated behind the White Sox dugout.

* * *

1950s: Clay Harper, manager of the minor-league St. Paul team, came out to argue a call. He became so infuriated that he accidentally spat his false teeth out onto the ground. Reassembling his composure, Harper bent down, picked up his errant teeth, and trotted back to the dugout.

* * *

1953: The first televised baseball brawl may have occurred on August 2, in a minor-league game between the Hollywood Stars and Los Angeles Angels. Ted Beard, trying to steal third, came in spikes high at third baseman Franklin, who responded by slugging Beard. Both teams joined in, and 50 police officers were called out.

Two weeks later, "The Brawl" was featured in *Life* magazine.

* * *

1954: Emmett Ashford, the first black umpire in the Major Leagues, recalled his first assignment in the Texas League, a night game between rivals El Paso and Chihuahua.

"When I walked into the park, I could hear the Texas crowd buzzing. Chihuahua has three Negroes, and when I called one safe in the second inning, the buzzing gets louder. In the fifth inning, a pitch that's a bit high on the home town player-manager Marv Williams, is a ball. But the catcher screams like Tarzan and pretty soon players from both teams are jawing their faces off around home plate, and I don't miss the dangerous meaning of that rumbling sound from the crowd. 'They'll kill you,' one Negro player said.

"Finally I raised my voice, and you know I can do that. After attaining the desired attention I deliver my ultimatum. 'Gentlemen,' I say, 'I realize I am in the sovereign state of Texas. I also realize my position is precarious and untenable.'

"'I say, gentlemen, this may be my last game as an umpire but I will run it my way. Now I am about to depart for the receptacle that contains new baseballs. When I return, if I find anyone here besides the catcher and the batter, I will throw you all out.'"

When Ashford returned, calm prevailed.

* * *

1961: A famous rhubarb occurred during the first week of the season. Leo Durocher, long a burr in umpires' sides, argued a call by Jocko Conlan, and Conlan threw him out. Durocher, never one to go quietly, kicked dirt on the umpire's trousers. Conlan tried to kick dirt back at Durocher, but, not wearing spikes, his foot skidded off the ground and kicked Durocher hard in the shin. Durocher kicked him back, Conlan returned the favor, and so it went.

Eventually a dim bulb flickered on in Durocher's skull. He remembered that umpires wore 1) shin guards beneath their pants, and 2) steel-toed shoes. Every time Jocko kicked Leo he raised a lump on Durocher's shin; every time Durocher kicked Conlan, he bruised his toe.

Durocher later wrote, "All at once it occurred to me that these were the lousiest odds I'd ever come up against."

* * *

Umpire George Majerkurth chewed tobacco and was not finicky about personal hygiene. Moreover he had a gap between his front teeth, and whenever he tried to talk and chew at the same time, he sprayed tobacco juice like a summer monsoon. This he did one day in mid-rhubarb with Leo Durocher, bathing him in brown expectoration. Enraged, Durocher leapt up and spat in Majerkurth's face.

Majerkurth roared like a wounded bear. "Oh, that's going to cost you $250 and ten days!"

"For what?!"

"You spat in my face."

"What the hell do you think this is—smallpox?"

"Mi-i-i-i-ine was an accident," Majerkurth sputtered.

Mimicking him, Durocher said, "Not mi-i-i-i-ine. Mi-i-i-i-ine was intentional."

38

For telling the truth," Majerkurth said, "if you get out of here fast, I won't fine you and I won't suspend you."

"Okay, Mage," Durocher said.

But before he left, Durocher kicked dirt over the umpire's pants and was fined $50 for that. Durocher's fans took up a collection to pay his fine. One day Durocher reached home plate for the pregame meeting with the umpires, and there on home plate was a sack filled with 5,000 pennies.

III. The Last Word

When they come out there, have the answers.

—Bill Klem

John McGraw may have been the rowdiest manager baseball has ever seen. Several times a season, National League president Young could expect a letter from McGraw that went something like this:

Dear Mr. Young:

Enclosed please find five dollars which I pay for the privilege of calling one of your umpires a stiff. I think he was a stiff on this particular occasion, but we all have our faults. Please acknowledge receipt and oblige. Kindly offer my regards to the umpire in question who compelled me to separate with the enclosed five spot.

*   *   *

In the nineteenth century, umpires worked alone, often calling pitches from behind the mound. Umpire Matty Fitzgerald, working solo one afternoon in Chicago, slipped extra baseballs inside his shirt.

As the pitcher went into his windup, Fitzgerald bent forward to watch the pitch. One of the spare balls dropped to the ground just as the pitcher cut loose. The batter lined a shot right back up the middle, and ball one struck ball two. One rolled toward shortstop, the other to the second baseman. Both infielders threw to first, where Frank McNichols gloved one throw and barehanded the other.

"Yer out!" Fitzgerald hollered. "Both balls beat you to the sack!"

* * *

Old-time umpire Tim Hurst, a fire-pluggish five-foot-five, was known for his firm and fearless decisions. One time Hurst was behind the plate with fiery John McGraw batting. When Hurst called strike two, he heard the usual grumbling from McGraw. The next pitch was called a ball.

"You blind so and so," McGraw fulminated. "It was right where the other one was."

Hurst feigned surprise. "Was it, Mugsy? Then strike three and yer out!"

* * *

Sometimes words failed Hurst, and that's when he got into trouble. Late in his cantankerous career, he picked up a beer mug thrown at him and heaved it back in the stands, badly injuring a fireman. Hurst was arrested, tried, convicted, and fined twenty dollars.

*   *   *

In contrast to the rough-and-tumble style of Hurst and other early umpires, National League umpire Bill Byron had a softer approach. Known as "Lord Byron, the Singing Umpire," he often responded to beefs over balls and strikes by singing a ditty he'd written just for the occasion.

Let me tell you something, son
Before you get much older
You cannot hit the ball, my friend
With the bat upon your shoulder.

*   *   *

Harry "Steamboat" Johnson umpired for 40 years, nearly all of them in the minors. Called Steamboat for his foghorn-like voice, he boosted his fame by writing his autobiography, *Standing the Gaff.*

He estimated that he made about a million decisions and had about four thousand bottles thrown his way—about 20 of which hit their target. He threw a few bottles back, but a fan in Memphis got the last word: He heaved Steamboat's autobiography at him, striking him in the head.

* * *

Umpire Bill Dineen was working first base one day when player-manager Jimmy Dykes took a long lead off first, then lapsed into reverie. A snap throw from the catcher awakened him and he dived desperately back to the bag. Before Dineen could make his call, Jimmy was screaming, "I made it! I made it!"

Dineen, fist already pointed skyward, looked down at Dykes. "You certainly did, Jimmy," he said soothingly, "but what detained you?"

* * *

In the late thirties, with Whitey Witt on first base, the batter hit a liner to the shortstop, who threw the ball into the stands trying to double up Witt at first. Umpire Bill Gutherie motioned Witt to second.

Whitey protested, "No, I get two bases—I should go to third."

Gutherie shook his head. "I'm giving you two bases. One dis way (pointing toward first) and one dat way (pointing toward second)."

*   *   *

Longtime umpire Bill Klem, though short in stature, was a giant on the field. Some would say a tyrant. During a rhubarb, he would often toe a line in the dirt and say, "Okay, yew applehead, cross dat line and yer out of da game!" Not many crossed it.

One of Klem's chief antagonists was fiery Frankie Frisch. As manager of the Pittsburgh Pirates, he was taunting Klem from the third-base coaching box one day. Klem ignored him until a Pittsburgh player was called out on strikes. Like a man suffering from a heart attack, Frisch let out a terrible cry of pain, clutched his chest, and toppled to the ground. He quivered, as though with fever, then stiffened like a corpse, his eyes fixed on the sky.

With that, Klem whipped off his mask and raced toward third, hollering, "If yer not dead when I get there, yer out of da game!"

* * *

1930s: After Frankie Frisch had argued a call with Klem, Johnny Mize of the Cardinals came to the plate. In the middle of the pitcher's windup, Klem decided he had more to say to Frisch. He was halfway to the on-deck circle when Mize roped a double. Giants manager Bill Terry argued it should be no pitch. Klem held his ground and allowed the double.

"Suppose . . ." Terry said, " . . . suppose the ball had gotten by Mize. What would you have called it then?"

"Why, I'd have called it what it was! Play ball!"

* * *

Frisch related another Klem moment, this time in Boston. At home plate before the game, Frisch pointed to the mounted cop out in left field, keeping the overflow crowd at bay. "How about the cop's horse?"

Frisch asked Klem. "Suppose he gets hit with the ball—I want a ground rule on him."

"Never mind the cop's horse," said Klem. "I'll take care of him."

About the third inning, a Pittsburgh hitter smacked a line drive down the leftfield foul line. The cop tried to dodge the ball, which whizzed right under the horse's belly. The runner slowed at third base, unsure what had happened, then tried to score and was thrown out at home.

As Frisch told the story: "Bill had run down the line, following the ball to see if there was any interference and I guess there wasn't any actually, but it was a good chance to holler."

"'How do you know the ball didn't hit the horse? You're getting so blind, I don't think you can even see the horse, let alone the ball.'

"He was so mad, he beat himself on the chest like Tarzan. 'How dare you say that to me.' he bellowed. 'I'm the king!'

"'The king!' I said. 'The king, my necktie!'

"He stuck his face right up against mine and said, 'Mr. Frisch, your necktie is in the clubhouse and if you hurry with your shower, in about two minutes you will be putting it on!'"

* * *

One hot afternoon, Frankie Frisch trotted from the coaching box to the dugout. When he passed umpire Beans Reardon, he slowed and said, "Beansie, I'm going into the cool of the dugout. I want to enjoy myself . . . have you a cigar perchance?"

"A cigar? What would I be doing with a cigar?"

"Well, you called that last play like a cigar store Indian, and I thought for sure you'd have one."

* * *

One day Klem drew a line in the dirt and dared Frankie Frisch to cross it. "Cross that line, yew applehead. That's all you got to do."

With that, Frisch wheeled about and sprinted straight toward Klem, skidding to a halt with his toes right on the line.

"Ohh, that's going to cost you, yew applehead. Now you've done it."

Meanwhile Leo Durocher had tiptoed around to the left, so that now he too was on the other side of the line. "And you're gone, too," Klem bellowed, pointing his mask toward the clubhouse. "Both of you, yewww appleheads!"

Durocher insisted that he'd gone around the line, not crossed it.

"Saaame thing," Klem intoned. "Saaaame difference. When I draw a line, it extends out to infinity."

*   *   *

One day Bill Klem ejected Pirate third baseman Pie Traynor. After the game, sportswriters hurried to the umpires' dressing room. This was news: Traynor never used bad language.

"Why was Traynor given the thumb?" a writer asked.

"He wasn't feeling well," Klem said.

"He looked okay before the game."

Klem shrugged. "Well, that's what he told me. He said he was sick of my stupid decisions."

* * *

After a close pitch, Hack Wilson stepped out of the batter's box. "You missed that one, Klem," he growled.

Klem snapped back, "If I'd had your bat in my hands, I wouldn't have."

* * *

After he was out of baseball, Leo Durocher wrote that umpire George Majerkurth was his favorite opponent. "The Maje wasn't a very good umpire, but he would always let you have your beef. I could get him so mad that his lower lip would turn blue and begin to quiver."

One day Durocher so infuriated Majerkurth, he looked as if he'd choke. They went jaw to jaw, Majerkurth looming over Durocher "like a big mastiff over a puppy."

"I'll reach down and bite your head off," Majerkurth growled.

Durocher's eyes brightened. "If you do," he said, "you'll have more brains in your stomach than you've got in your head."

*   *   *

Working the plate one day, umpire Bill McGowan made several close calls that went against the Washington Senators, incurring the wrath of coach Nick Altrock. In the sixth inning, a foul ball rocketed into the stands. When the inning ended, McGowan noticed a woman being carried off on a stretcher.

As Altrock went by, McGowan asked if the ball had hit her.

"No," he said, "you called that last one right and she fainted."

*   *   *

Bobby Thompson, who hit the famous 1951 home run to give the Giants the pennant, once told Augie Donatelli that he was the only ump who ever threw him out of a game.

"My honor was at stake," Donatelli explained.

"Your honor! I bet you don't even remember what happened."

"Sure I do. I called a strike on you and you called me a _____."

"Yeah," said Thompson, "but why did you put me out for that? Nobody heard it but you, me, and the catcher."

"I know, but I didn't want the catcher going through life thinking I was a _____."

*   *   *

One day National League umpire Dusty Boggess called catcher Clyde McCullough out on strikes. "You missed that one," McCullough said. "That was a ball."

"You know, Mac, for twenty years as a player, I too thought that was a ball. But it's a strike—so I went into umpiring."

As the first African American to umpire in the Major
Leagues, Emmett Ashford needed more than good
judgment. Blessed with a quick mind and tongue, he could
usually dance around trouble. "You learn to build up
defenses like a nightclub comedian against drunks," he
said. "When somebody calls you 'porter' and says, 'Hey,
pick up my bags,' you just tell him, 'I would, sir, but
they're attached to your eyes.'"

*   *   *

In 1970, after five years in the big leagues, after working
one All-Star game and one World Series, Emmett Ashford
retired with a $1,600-a-year pension. "It hasn't been easy
being an umpire and Negro too," he said. "But it could've
been worse. It'd be even harder for Sammy Davis, Jr. He
only has one eye."

*   *   *

On July 5, 1970, Dock Ellis of the Pirates was pitching to
Paul Popovich of the Cubs, who hit a grounder to first
baseman Al Oliver, about 20 feet from the bag. When Ellis
didn't cover, Oliver had to race Popovich to the base
himself.

Both men arrived at the same time. As they collided, Oliver was thrown into umpire Tom Gorman, who was set up on one knee in foul territory. When the dust settled, Gorman was on the ground. He'd had the wind knocked out of him and couldn't speak. (He also had a broken leg but didn't know it.)

As Gorman lay there, eyes closed, struggling to catch his breath, he heard a familiar voice. "Did he call him out or did he call him safe?"

It was Cubs manager Leo Durocher talking to Pirates manager Danny Murtaugh. Leo the Lip, Gorman's longtime nemesis.

"What's the call? Did he make a call?"

After a moment, still struggling for air, Gorman was able to croak, "Who's talking?"

"It's me, Leo," the voice said.

"Well, if it's Leo, he's out."

*   *   *

Ron Luciano was umpiring behind the plate when Sal Bando stepped into the box. Mired in a deep slump, Bando begged for help. "Ronnie, what the hell am I doing wrong?"

"I got no idea," said Luciano, "but it looks like you're a lot further from the plate than you used to be."

The next night, Bando hit a long home run. As he approached third base, he screamed, "That was it, Ron! That was it!"

Luciano, grinning, reached out and shook Bando's hand.

When Baltimore manager Earl Weaver complained that Luciano was now coaching players on how to beat his team, the umpire offered this defense: "I was happy for the poor guy."

*   *   *

Bill Kinnamon, chief instructor of the umpire school I attended in 1975, loved to tell this story. "It was a hot night in Kansas City, really muggy. I'm working first base when suddenly we get this invasion of flies. Big ol' nasty horse-flies buzzing into our eyes and ears.

"I have a couple of close ones that go against Kansas City, and I start to hear it from some chisel-mouthed lady in the stands. 'You stink! You're rotten clear through! You couldn't umpire a cat fight!'

"Back at first, here come the flies again. I'm swattin' at 'em and swattin' at 'em, when suddenly I hear her, at the top of her lungs: 'Don't bother to swat them away! They always hang around a horse's ass!'"

*　*　*

My mentor, Willie Rossi, took credit for this last word, though it has also been attributed to Bill Klem. Willie, working the plate one day, was roasted for five innings by a serpent-tongued woman in the first row. He suffered in silence until, in full-throated disagreement with one of his calls, she leapt to her feet and shrieked, "If I was your wife, I'd give you poison!"

Seeing his opening, Willie removed his mask and approached the backstop. In a measured tone, he said, "Lady, if I was your husband, I'd take that poison."

*　*　*

In one of his first games in the National League, umpire Bruce Froemming worked behind catcher Tom Haller. For several innings, Haller questioned every close pitch, testing the rookie umpire but never getting abusive.

Finally he said, "Bruce, what's your last name?"

"Froemming."

"How do you spell it?"

"F-R-O-E-M-M-I-N-G."

"That's with one I?"

Froemming raised one eyebrow. "Yeah . . .?"

"That's what I thought. That's how you been calling them all night."

IV. My Last Word

With few exceptions, umpires don't have statisticians—or even fans. No one records their ERA or BA, or compiles highlights of their greatest moments. If, however, anyone ever compiled the highlights of American League umpire Nestor Chylak's career, the following play would be a centerpiece.

It occurred on the big stage—the 1960 World Series between the Yankees and Pirates. Yogi Berra was batting with Mickey Mantle on first. Chylak was umpiring at first.

Berra roped a line drive down the first-base line. While Mantle scrambled back to first, Pirate first baseman Rocky Nelson dived and short-hopped the ball near the bag.

Suddenly Chylak stood all alone in the spotlight. In quick succession, he: 1) pointed toward the infield to signal fair ball; 2) skinned the back of his arm, indicating Nelson had trapped the ball; 3) pointed at Berra and thrust up his right arm, signaling that Nelson had touched first before Berra; and 4) signaled safe, meaning that Mantle had slid safely back ahead of Nelson's tag.

Four calls in 2.3 seconds. Maybe the greatest ever. The crowd, stunned, remained silent for a moment, as though needing time to parse a play of such complexity. Then a few fans stood and cheered, ripples of applause spreading, then swelling into a great roar.

Of course, Chylak is not alone. Every day of every season, all over the world, umpires are hustling into position, showing good judgment, and getting 'em right. Silence is their applause. But maybe next time you see an umpire excel, armed as you are now with a better eye and higher awareness, you'll be more inclined to say, "Nice game, ump!"

V. Notable Moments in Umpiring History

*If they did get a machine to replace us,
you know what would happen to it?
Why, the players would bust it to pieces
every time it ruled against them.
They'd clobber it with a bat.*

–National League umpire Harry Wendelstadt

August 22, 1886: In the eleventh inning of a game between the Cincinnati Reds and the Louisville Colonels, outfielder Abner Powell went back on a deep fly ball—and was attacked by a dog. The mongrel latched onto Powell's leg like it was a soup bone. By the time Powell freed himself, the batter had circled the bases with the winning run.

Do the modern rules mention canine interference?

*   *   *

Circa 1890: In a game in Louisville, John McGraw hooked his fingers inside the belt of runner Pete Browning, who was attempting to tag and score from third on a fly ball. Browning, forewarned of McGraw's antics, undid his buckle and tore for the plate, leaving McGraw holding the belt.

Should McGraw have been ejected?

* * *

May 6, 1892: Umpire Jack Sheridan stopped play between the scoreless Cincinnati and Boston teams in the fourteenth inning because the sun was at such an angle that it simultaneously blinded both the batter and pitcher. It was possibly the only time in baseball history that a game was called on account of sun.

What criteria should umpires use in calling a game?

* * *

August 7, 1906: The New York Giants forfeited a game to Chicago when manager John McGraw locked umpire James Johnston out of the ballpark. McGraw, who believed he "wasn't getting a fair shake" from Johnston, sent out one of his own players to umpire. The move was disallowed by the league president.

Can an umpire eject a manager from outside the stadium?

* * *

1907: Dave Altizer, shortstop for the Chicago White Sox, enjoyed a reputation as a practical joker. One time, at least, his teammates got him back. During a game with Cleveland, Altizer walked with one out. Stealing on the first pitch, he put his head down and raced for second, unaware that the ball had been lined to the first baseman who'd stepped on first for an inning-ending double play.

Third-base coach Nick Altrock saw that Altizer had no idea what had happened. He also saw opportunity. "Slide, Dave! Slide!" he cried.

Altizer slid beautifully into second base.

Just as he looked up, the Cleveland first baseman, who had figured out the joke, heaved the ball wildly into leftfield. Coach Altrock urged Altizer to get up and join him at third. Dave charged down the line and executed a magnificent slide just as the ball, intentionally overthrown, shot over the base and rolled toward the stands.

Altizer again got to his feet and raced toward home. The catcher, ball in hand, was waiting for him, but he intentionally missed the tag.

"Yer out!" cried the umpire.

Altizer erupted in protest. "You blind son of a bitch! He missed me by two feet!"

"You dumb son of a bitch!" the umpire retorted. "You were out at first base!"

When and why should an umpire stop play?

*   *   *

September 4, 1908: With runners on second and third, Detroit's Germany Schaefer, who was on second, attempted to steal first! At the time this was legal, an accepted ploy to confuse the catcher and try to score the runner from third. The rule was soon changed to outlaw running the bases in reverse order.

What's the call if someone does run the bases in reverse order?

*   *   *

September 23, 1908: New York Giants player Fred Merkle became infamous for this play, known eponymously as "Merkle's Boner." Merkle was on first base when Al Bridwell hit what appeared to be the game-winning single against the Cubs. As the "winning" run scored from third, Merkle ran halfway to second, then turned and headed for the clubhouse. With thousands of fans milling about on the field, Cubs second baseman Johnny Evers called for the ball and tagged second. Umpire Hank O'Day ruled Merkle out and disallowed the run. The Giants filed a protest, and the entire game was replayed two weeks later with the Cubs winning the game and the pennant.

Why, according to the rule book, did Merkle have to tag second?

* * *

July 17, 1914: While legging out a triple, New York Giants outfielder Red Murray was struck by lightning, which felled him like a tree between second and third base. While lying there stunned, he was tagged out.

Should an umpire ever call time to protect an injured player? Is time ever automatically out?

* * *

June 8, 1920: Reds centerfielder Ed Roush was ejected for taking a nap in the outfield. While his manager was arguing a call with umpire Bill Klem, Roush stretched out on the grass and fell asleep.

Should he have been ejected for delay of game?

* * *

July 26, 1935: New York's Jesse Hill hit into an unusual double play. His vicious line drive ricocheted off the head of Washington pitcher Ed Linke and flew back to catcher Jack Redmond, who caught it and threw to second to double off the runner who had failed to tag up.

When could the runner legally tag up and advance?

*   *   *

August 13, 1935: During a game in Cincinnati, the crowd became so unruly that a melee seemed likely. Umpire Beans Reardon tried to calm them with a personal speech that backfired. League president Ford Frick fined and reprimanded the umpires, and in so doing set the policy that exists today: The home team polices its stands and the umpires stay out of it.

Why is it best that the umpires stay out of it?

*   *   *

February 1950: Bill Bundy of the Hollywood Stars, trying to score, was knocked unconscious at home plate when he ran into the catcher. As the catcher searched for the ball, the on-deck batter took Bundy's hand and placed it on home plate.

Is that legal?

* * *

June 3, 1956: Nellie Fox of the Chicago White Sox was hit by two different pitches on the same at-bat. The first time Fox was nailed by Orioles pitcher Johnny Schmitz, the plate umpire ruled he'd made no attempt to get out of the way and thus did not get first base.

What must a batter do to be awarded first base?

* * *

June 7, 1957: A Brooklyn version of London's famed "pea soup" settled on Ebbets Field, forcing the umpires to call the game on account of fog.

When is a lot of fog too much fog?

June 23, 1963: Jimmy Piersall celebrated his one hundredth Major League home run by circling the bases "back-first."

Should the run count? What if he'd run the bases in reverse order?

*   *   *

July 29, 1965: In a Yankees-Twins game, the umpires took away an RBI single from Yankee catcher Thurman Munson when they found pine tar more than 18 inches up his bat handle.

What's the current rule on pine tar?

*   *   *

April 10, 1974: Nick Bremigan, my instructor at umpire school, told this story about his first plate game in the American League. Right from the first inning, he began to hear chipping from the darkest recesses of the Chicago dugout. "A distinctive voice with a bad attitude," Bremigan said.

About the third inning, crew chief Nestor Chylak sidled down to calm Bremigan. "The guy roasting you is wearing a white towel around his neck," he said helpfully.

Three pitches later, Bremigan heard the voice again—"How can you sleep with all these lights on?" Reacting swiftly, Bremigan yanked off his mask, faced the Chicago dugout, and intoned, "You with the white towel around your neck! One more word and you're gone!"

Silence reigned—for about five pitches. Then: "You could screw up a one-car funeral!"

Again Bremigan responded with great command, ripping off his mask and taking a step or two toward the Chicago dugout. There, to his horror, he saw 25 guys wearing white towels around their necks.

What should Bremigan have done differently?

*   *   *

June 4, 1974: The umpires were forced to forfeit a game in Cleveland on 10-cent beer night. In the ninth inning with the score tied, unruly fans came onto the field and disrupted the game.

At what point should umpires forfeit a game?

*   *   *

1976: At Milwaukee's County Stadium, the Braves were trailing 9-6 in the bottom of the ninth with the bases loaded. Just before Dave Pagan delivered the pitch to Don Money, first baseman Chris Chambliss asked umpire Jim McKean for time out. McKean sprinted toward home waving his arms, but he was too late. The pitch was hammered into the bleachers for what appeared to be a dramatic 10-9 home-team victory. The fans went wild and the players ran off the field.

Some were half-undressed in the locker room before they got the word—grand slam nullified. A do-over. Money returned to the plate, hit a sacrifice fly, and Milwaukee lost 9-7.

When should umpires change their calls?

May 27, 1981: Mets' third baseman Lenny Randle got down on his hands and knees to blow a slow roller foul.

Foul ball? Interference?

* * *

May 4, 1984: Oakland slugger Dave Kingman hit a towering pop fly that got stuck in the roof of the Metrodome.

Ground-rule double? Home run? Out?

* * *

July 1, 2005: On this day the same batter completed two full at-bats consecutively. The problem started when Kansas City manager Buddy Bell gave the umpires a different lineup than the one he posted in the dugout. In the first inning, David DeJesus led off with a single. Angels manager Mike Scioscia then showed umpire Jerry Crawford his lineup card (the official lineup card), which said that Angel Berroa should hit first.

What's the penalty for batting out of order? Who bats next?

September 14, 2005: With Gabe Kapler on first, Tony Graffanino homered. While rounding second base, Kapler crumpled with a leg injury. Graffanino stopped and stayed behind Kapler until Boston manager Terry Francona could pinch-run for Kapler.

Is that legal? Place the runners.

* * *

April 16, 2006: In a game between the Orioles and Angels, Miguel Tejada was on first with no outs. Javie Lopez hit a long fly ball to center. The centerfielder leaped at the fence but came up empty. He hit the wall so hard, he fell to the ground, the wind knocked out of him. In the meantime, Tejada, thinking the ball has been caught, headed back to first and was passed by Lopez, who correctly assumed it was a home run.

Who's out? Who scores?

Photo Courtesy of UPI

VI. You Make the Call

*They expect an umpire to be perfect on Opening Day
and to improve as the season goes on.*

—American League umpire Nestor Chylak

Umpires must know the rules and be able to apply them
quickly. Here's your chance to rule on some tough plays
without fear of inciting a riot. What's more, you can take
as much time as you need. For positioning questions,
assume that two umpires are on the field. The answers
follow.

1. Runner on first base is stealing. As the batter swings at
the pitch, his bat contacts the catcher's mitt.

2. With a runner on second, batter hits a bouncer to shortstop. The runner, moving toward third, has to slow to
avoid being hit by the batted ball. The ball, in fact, just
misses the runner, and the shortstop kicks it for an error.

3. Runner on first and a ground ball to the second
baseman. The throw to first goes into the dugout.

4. Batter hits a foul fly ball near the visitor's bench. First baseman moves over, makes the catch in live territory, then his momentum carries him across the chalk line separating live and dead territory.

5. With the bases empty, batter hits a ground ball to short. When the throw takes the first baseman off the bag, he attempts to sweep-tag the batter-runner.

6. Runners on second and third, and a fly ball to center. Both runners tag and move up one base. The defense appeals that both runners left too early.

7. Runner on first is stealing and gets caught in a rundown. While in the baseline, the runner turns and contacts a fielder who does not have the ball.

8. Runner on first, fly ball to deep leftfield. Runner, thinking the ball will be caught, retreats to first to tag. As the ball hits off the fielder's glove, the batter-runner rounds first, passing the tagging runner.

9. No runners on base and a sinking liner to centerfield. The outfielder charges and either makes the catch or short-hops it—it's tough to tell.

10. Bases loaded, no outs, and a pop fly to the shortstop.

11. Bases loaded, no outs. A fly ball is hit to the outfield that looks like it will fall in. The runners take off, but the centerfielder makes a sliding catch for out # 1. He throws the ball to second to catch the runner off base for out # 2. The ball is then thrown to first to catch the last runner off base for out # 3. The runner from third base, who never tagged up, touched home plate before the final out was made at first. Does the run count?

12. The lead runner gets in a rundown between third and home. When he makes it safely back to third, he finds his teammate, the batter-runner, already there on the bag. The defense tags both runners while they are standing on third base.

Answers

1. Ask yourself, "Who screwed up?" Answer: the defense. Since the offense may benefit more from the play than the penalty, let the play go. Do not call time immediately. If the batter and all runners advance at least one base, ignore the interference. If not, call time and enforce the penalty: the batter gets first base. But do any runners advance? Consult your rulebook, as this part of the rule varies by level of play.

2. No interference. The runner must avoid being hit by a batted ball, lest he be called out for interference. That may require slowing down or speeding up, which is sometimes enough to distract a fielder. Unless the runner did something intentional or out of the ordinary to interfere with the fielder, let the play go and call nobody out.

3. As soon as the ball enters dead territory, the plate umpire should raise both arms and yell, "Dead ball." Any partners should mimic the call, stopping any hell-bent runners. Repeat as necessary. Then, immediately and with great command, make your awards, pointing the runners to their allotted bases. And know those awards cold.

Throws that go out of play (except from a pitcher on the rubber) are always two-base awards. It's simply a matter of whether the award is made from the base attained at the time of the pitch or at the time of the release. Consult the rulebook for the particular sport.

4. As soon as the fielder carries the caught ball into dead territory, the plate umpire should raise both arms and cry, "Dead ball!" Then immediately and forcefully award any runners one base beyond the base they had at the time of the pitch.

5. With no runners on, the plate umpire should move up the first-base line, halfway if possible. The base umpire makes the initial call at first, but if you don't see it well and if one team erupts, consider going to your partner for help. If you do that, it's best to go immediately and forcefully: "Did he get him?!" And the plate ump's reply should be in an equally stentorian tone—"Yes, he did!" —synchronized with an aggressive out call. Put all those pieces together—hustling plate umpire, dynamic communication, and, if necessary, quick reversal—and the umpire crew comes out of a tough situation looking very good indeed.

6. First, the defense can indeed appeal both bases. With few exceptions, the base umpire is responsible for watching the touches and tags at first and second base; the plate umpire has third and home. If a runner leaves too soon or misses a bag, the umpires say nothing unless the defense properly appeals. The pitcher must put the ball in play. Once that is accomplished without a balk, the appropriate umpire makes the call. You should have been in position to see it, but if you weren't, call the runners safe. Never guess "out."

7. Obstruction. Ask yourself, who screwed up? Answer: the defense. Since the offense may benefit more from the play than the penalty, delay calling time. But most often, the play grinds to a halt, and everyone turns to the umpire for clarity. Now call time, yell, "Obstruction!" and make awards. Consult your rulebook, as some levels of play always advance the runner while others award the base to which the runner was heading—in this case, first base.

8. Who screwed up? Answer: the offense. Normally, if the offense errs, you kill the play immediately, under the assumption that the offense may not benefit from the play. This play is an exception. Immediately raise your right arm, point to the batter-runner, and call him out.

But do not raise both arms and kill the play unless that is the third out of the inning. Otherwise, let the play go, as the tagging runner may still advance or be thrown out.

9. In the two-umpire system, with the bases empty, the plate umpire should hustle out into fair territory, generally toward the ball but at an angle to maximize his view. On a close catch/no-catch, make the call as quickly as possible, selling it with voice and flair. If one side erupts in anger, consider taking your partner aside for a conference. If your partner saw it no better than you did, stick with the original call.

10. The infield fly rule is in effect. Call the batter out, but don't call time out. Delay the out call a moment if you have any doubt whether the ball can be caught "with ordinary effort." (Note: ordinary effort varies greatly according to skill level.) Once the plate umpire decides, yes, it can be caught with ordinary effort (and the defense dropping it does not necessarily make that a bad decision), he should raise his right arm, making the out call, while shouting, "Batter is out!" two or more times. The base umpire should mimic the out call. If the pop fly is then dropped, both umpires should repeat the out call loudly. Remember, time is not out. The runners can advance at their own risk, although they must tag up if the ball is caught.

11. Depends. The rules allow for a "fourth out" that would disallow the run—but only if the defense properly appeals the runner leaving third too soon. If the defense doesn't appeal, the run counts.

12. The batter-runner is out. The lead runner has the right to a base until he abandons it once and for all.

True/False

1. If the third out of an inning is the result of a force play, no runs score on the play.

2. When the batter interferes with the catcher's throw to second, the umpire should call the stealing runner out.

3. During batter's interference, there is no penalty if the catcher throws out the stealing runner.

4. Umpires should never change their calls.

5. A runner is out for going more than 3 feet out of the baseline only if he does so to avoid a tag.

6. On the field, an umpire should never anticipate.

7. While moving into position to make a call, the umpire should always keep both eyes on the ball.

8. A good umpire will sometimes let a beefing ballplayer have the last word.

9.   With a runner on first and one out, a fly ball is hit to rightfield for the second out. The runner is almost to second, and the throw to first to double him off sails into the stands. The proper award is the base the runner was going to (first) plus the next base (second).

10. The umpire has the right to rule on any point not specifically covered in the rule book.

Answers

1. True.

2. False. The batter is out.

3. True

4. False. If the call involves a misinterpreted rule and the umpires catch it in time, they must change the call to avoid a possible protest. With few exceptions, umpires will not change judgment calls.

5. True.

6. False. For umpires, there is good anticipation and bad anticipation. *Do not* anticipate out or safe, ball or strike. *Do* anticipate how a play will develop and where to go on the field.

7. False. The umpire's mantra: Watch the ball, glance at the runner.

8. True.

9. True.

10. False. The award is two bases. Depending on the level of baseball, awards are made from the base the runners had attained either at time of pitch or time of release.

VII. So You Think You Know Baseball

Harry Simmons was a baseball executive with a love for baseball history, rules, and statistics. While working in minor-league baseball, he held regular conferences with umpires to discuss rules and review knotty problems. He started to compile those odd plays, and in 1949 submitted several of them to the *Saturday Evening Post* under the title "So You Think You Know Baseball." The series ran until 1961, and later was published in *Baseball Digest*, where I re-read them.

With a bow to Harry Simmons, here are six plays, edited slightly, from the series "So You Think You Know Baseball."

1. Cincinnati is leading San Francisco 1-0 as the Giants bat in the fifth at Riverfront Stadium. Johnny LeMaster singles and steals second. Jack Clark walks, putting runners on first and third. As the Reds' pitcher goes into his stretch, LeMaster breaks for the plate.

The pitcher recognizes the attempted steal before he starts his windup. He backs completely off the rubber and throws the ball home. LeMaster is sure to be out, but the batter slashes at the ball and singles to right.

How would you rule?

2. Top of the eighth at Los Angeles, with the Braves leading the Dodgers 6 to 1. Bruce Benedict opens with a spanking single to left. The next hitter lifts a pop up to Steve Sax near second base. The batter-runner tosses his bat in disgust and jogs toward first.

Sax, under the pop, notices the Braves hitter's lazy pace. He lets the ball drop at his feet, traps it, and throws to first. First baseman Greg Brock tags Benedict, who is still standing on first, then touches the bag before the batter-runner does.

The Dodgers claim double-play. The Braves maintain a runner in such circumstances cannot be put out while standing on a base. How would you call it?

3. The Cincinnati Reds are at bat against the Expos in the seventh inning of a 2-2 tie game. Ken Griffey is hit by a pitch and goes to third on Joe Morgan's double to right. With runners on second and third, Montreal wants to intentionally walk the next batter, Johnny Bench. But the first three balls the Montreal pitcher throws are all nearly wild pitches.

The Montreal manager instructs his pitcher to stand on the rubber and not pitch for a full minute. Then, he reasons, the umpire will have to call ball four. Is that the call you'd make?

4. The Phillies are batting in the top of the sixth at windy Candlestick Park. With one out, Gary Maddox singles and moves to second when Manny Trillo is hit by a pitch. Larry Bowa then lifts a high pop fly to short rightfield.

As the rightfielder moves in on the ball, a strong gust of wind sweeps it back toward the infield. It comes down just beyond the base path. The Giants outfielder waves off the first baseman, who could have made an easy catch, and dives desperately for the ball. It lands safely and skips toward the outfield.

Bowa ends up at second and Maddox and Trillo score. Or do they?

5. Dodgers and Reds are tied 2 to 2 in the top of the sixth inning. Ron Cey singles to left. The Reds pitcher, on his first offering to Steve Garvey, flinches just before delivering the pitch.

The umpires immediately call "balk," but Garvey slashes at the pitch and drives a single to right.

While Garvey stops safely at first base, Cey rounds second and tries for third. He's cut down by a fine throw from Reds outfielder Cesar Geronimo.

Is Cey out? You make the call.

6. With a runner on first base, National League umpires stand between the mound and second base.

In the first inning at Houston, Dan Gladden opens the Giants attack with a sharp single to right. Then Jeffrey Leonard ropes one back up the middle. The ball skips cleanly by the pitcher and heads for the umpire. He leaps to avoid it, but it strikes the heel of his shoe and right into the glove of second baseman Bill Doran of the Astros. Doran flips the ball to shortstop Craig Reynolds for a force out of Gladden.

What's the call?

Answers

1. The batter is out for interference. Once the pitcher backed off the rubber, he is treated as an infielder. Section 8.01e of the *Official Baseball Rules* says, *"If the pitcher removes his pivot foot from contact with the pitcher's plate by stepping backward with that foot, he thereby becomes an infielder."*

Note: With fewer than two outs, LeMaster, not the batter, is out. Section 7.08g: *"Any base runner is out when he attempts to score on a play in which the batter interferes with the play at home base before two are out."*

2. It's a double play. Because a force play was created when Sax trapped the ball, Benedict is no longer entitled to first base. The procedure must be exact, however. Had Brock touched the base before tagging Benedict, the force would have been removed and Benedict would not be out.

Section 2.00: *"A force play is a play in which a runner legally loses his right to occupy a base by reason of the batter becoming a base runner."*

3. Call a balk, not a ball. It's a ball only when the bases are empty. If runners are on base, *"it is a balk when the pitcher unnecessarily delays the game."* [Section 8.05h] Each runner moves up one base. The count on Bench remains 3-0.

4 Maddox and Trillo score, but Bowa is out under the infield fly rule. Section 2.00 of the Official Baseball Rules: *"An infield fly is a fair fly ball . . . which can be caught by an infielder with ordinary effort, when first and second, or first, second and third bases are occupied before two are out."*

Since the ball *could have* been caught with ordinary effort, Bowa should have been called out before the ball hit the ground. The ball is alive and runners may advance at their own risk.

5. Disregard the balk. Cey is out. Section 8.05b of the Official Baseball Rules offers this penalty for a balk: *"The ball is dead and each runner shall advance one base without liability to be put out, unless the batter reaches first base on a hit . . . and all other runners advance at least one base, in which case the play proceeds without reference to the balk."*

6. No one is out. Place Gladden on second base and Leonard on first, and credit Leonard with a base hit.

When a batted ball strikes an umpire before passing an infielder (except the pitcher), the ball is instantly dead and runners hold their bases or advance one base if necessary to make room for the batter-runner. [Section 5.09f ; 6.08d]

VIII. Quotes by and About Umpires

The umpire must be quick witted. He may not, like the wise old owl of the bench, look over his gold-rimmed eyeglasses, inform the assembled multitude that he will "take the matter under advisement," and then adjourn the court for a week or two to satisfy himself how he ought to decide. No, indeed. He must be johnny-on-the-spot with a decision hot off the griddle and he must stick to it, right or wrong—or be lost. –A.G. Spaulding in America's National Game (1911)

The best thing about umpiring is seeing the best in baseball every day. The cardinal rule of umpiring is to follow the ball wherever it goes. Well, if you watch the ball, you can't help seeing somebody make a great catch . . . That's what makes umpiring so much fun. –National League umpire Shag Crawford

You argue with the umpire because there is nothing else you can do about it. –Leo Durocher

As a whole, the managers today are different in temperament. Most have very good communication skills and are more understanding of the umpire's job. That doesn't mean they are better managers. It just means that I perceive today's managers a bit differently. –Major League umpire Jim Evans

Professional managers, coaches, and players have a right to question an umpire's decision if they do it in a professional manner. When they become personal, profane, or violent, they have crossed the line and must be dealt with accordingly. –Jim Evans

Most plays that are missed by the umpire are caused by the umpire not reading those cues early enough and making the proper adjustments. –Jim Evans

Take pride in your work at all times. Remember, respect for an umpire is created off the field as well as on. –Ford Frick

One of the really wrong theories about officiating is that a good official is one you never notice. The umpire who made that statement was probably a real poor official who tried to get his paycheck and hide behind his partners and stay out of trouble all his life. Control of the ballgame is the difference between umpires that show up for the players and the managers. –National League umpire Bruce Froemming

It isn't enough for an umpire merely to know what he's doing. He has to look as though he knows what he's doing too. –National League umpire Larry Goetz

Boys, I'm one of those umpires that misses 'em every once in a while so if it's close, you'd better hit it. –Cal Hubbard

Being an umpire wasn't such a tough job. You really have to understand only two things and that's maintaining discipline and knowing the rule book. –Cal Hubbard

Umpire's heaven is a place where he works third base every game. Home is where the heartache is. –American League umpire Ron Luciano

Any umpire who claims he never missed a call is . . . well, an umpire. –Ron Luciano

Umpires are human, too—as we are finding out. –Steve Lyons

Why is it they boo me when I call a foul ball correctly and they applaud the starting pitcher when he gets taken out of the ballgame? –American League umpire Jerry Neudecker

Fans and players boo and abuse umpires, but there isn't one umpire in the history of baseball who has ever been proved guilty of being dishonest. I've very proud to have been an umpire. –American League umpire George Pipgras

Wanting to be an umpire is tantamount to wanting to be President of the United States. I can admire their fierce sense of responsibility, whether they are right or wrong, but sometimes it comes down to being a thankless job; however, the job must be done. –Art Rust in *Recollections of a Baseball Junkie* (1985)

The worst thing about umpiring [in professional baseball] is the loneliness. It's a killer. Every city is a strange city. You don't have a home. Ballplayers are home fifty percent of the time, umpires are not. –American League umpire Ernie Stewart

The thing that surprised me most in baseball is the amount of integrity that most umpires have. It actually took me a while to believe what a good game they'd give you the next night after a blow-up. –Earl Weaver

Photo Courtesy of National Baseball Library

Bill Klem Quotes

Bill Klem, often touted as the greatest umpire ever, may also have been the most quotable arbiter. Here is a sampling of his remarks.

An angry player can't argue with the back of an umpire who is walking away.

Baseball is more than a game to me, it's a religion.

Fix your eye on the ball from the moment the pitcher holds it in his glove. Follow it as he throws to the plate and stay with it until the play is completed. Action takes place only where the ball goes.

Gentleman, he was out because I said he was out. (Statement made after being shown a photo of a blown call.)

It ain't nothin' till I call it.

That guy in a twenty-five cent bleacher seat is as much entitled to know a call as the guy in the boxes. He can see my arm signal even if he can't hear my voice.

The best umpired game is the game in which the fans cannot recall the umpires who worked it.

The most cowardly thing in the world is blaming mistakes upon the umpires. Too many managers strut around on the field trying to manage the umpires instead of their teams.

There are one-hundred fifty-four games in a season and you can find one-hundred fifty-four reasons why your team should have won every one of them.

Your job is to umpire for the ball and not the player.

Resources

Suggested Reading

How to Umpire Baseball and Softball: An Introduction to Basic Umpiring Skills
Steve Boga

The definitive how-to-umpire book. The companion to the author's instructional DVD, *You Be the Judge.*

The Umpire Strikes Back
Ron Luciano

Humorous observations about the umpiring life.

The Fall of the Roman Umpire
Ron Luciano

More humorous observations about the umpiring life.

The Best Seat in Baseball but You Have to Stand: The Game as the Umpires See It
Lee Gutkind

An account of the author's travels with a National League umpire crew during the 1974 season.

The Men in Blue: Conversations with Umpires
Larry R. Gerlach

Major League umpires up close and personal.

As They See 'Em: A Fan's Travels in the Land of Umpires
Bruce Weber

A baseball devotee goes to an umpire school and then wherever umpire stories take him.

Strrr-ike!!: Emmett Ashford, Major League Umpire
Adrienne Cherie Ashford

The life story of the first black umpire in the Major Leagues, as told by his daughter.

Online Resources

http://www.howtoumpirebaseball.com
The author's website, which includes links to instructional materials as well as chapters from his memoir, *Dress Blues and Tennis Shoes*, about two umpires' struggles in the Texas League.

http://mlb.mlb.com/mlb/official_info/umpires/roster.jsp
Everything you want to know about Major League umpires.

http://www.naso.org/BeOfficial/sportspages/baseball.html
This National Association of Sports Officials (NASO) site is the starting place for officials in most amateur sports, including baseball and softball.

http://web.minorleaguebaseball.com/milb/info/umpires.jsp?mc=_ump_history
Umpiring in the minor leagues revealed.

http://www.majorleagueumpires.com/umpire_schools.htm
All about the umpire schools for professional baseball.

http://www.collegiatebaseball.com/umpiring/umpirelinks.htm
Full of links to sites about umpires and umpiring.

http://www.sdabu.com/history_main.htm
An engaging history of umpiring.

DVD

You Be the Judge: An Introduction to Basic Umpire Skills
Steve Boga, producer/writer

The companion to the author's instructional book, *How to Umpire Baseball and Softball: An Introduction to Basic Umpiring Skills.* **You Be the Judge** is the best umpire training DVD available for all levels of baseball and softball officials. It's ideal for both umpires and for umpire trainers.